Then & Now

WEST ROXBURY

from Cathy & Kelley

christmas 2005

Cass's Corner, pictured at the end of the 19th century, is the junction of Centre and Spring Streets and lies directly opposite the site of the Second Church in Roxbury, which was established in 1712 and was located at Church Street in 1773. Centre and South Streets, two of the oldest streets in the neighborhood, connected the area to Dedham.

Then & Now
WEST ROXBURY

Anthony Mitchell Sammarco

ARCADIA

First published 2003

Published by Arcadia Publishing,
an imprint of Tempus Publishing Inc.
Portsmouth NH, Charleston SC, Chicago,
San Francisco

Printed in Great Britain

Library of Congress Catalog Card Number: 2003108331

For all general information, contact Arcadia Publishing:
Telephone 843-853-2070
Fax 843-853-0044
E-mail sales@arcadiapublishing.com
For customer service and orders:
Toll-free 1-888-313-2665

Visit us on the Internet at www.arcadiapublishing.com

For Anthony Bognanno

In this early-20th-century view, languidly posing for the photographer are two gentlemen in a canoe on the Charles River at the Vine Rock Bridge, with its stone arches creating a visually interesting background. The bucolic quality of the Charles River has always created a picturesque and interesting area that, in many cases, remains undeveloped and protected to this day.

CONTENTS

The Parental School was established by the city of Boston as a reform school for truant boys and was located on Spring Street in West Roxbury. The red-brick and granite Romanesque Revival building was designed by Edmund March Wheelwright (1854–1912), who served as Boston city architect from 1891 to 1895 and "set a high level for municipal architecture in the United States." The building was used as an army hospital during World War I. Today, the site is the West Roxbury Department of Veterans Affairs Medical Center. (Author's collection.)

INTRODUCTION

West Roxbury . . . is a hometown which the larger city cannot engulf.

—From an early-20th-century flier

Originally a part of Roxbury, the neighborhood of West Roxbury was known as the Westerly End, versus the Jamaica End, or what became known as Jamaica Plain, of Roxbury. The area of present-day West Roxbury is today a thriving neighborhood bounded by Roslindale, Brookline, the Charles River, and Dedham. It was incorporated as an independent town in reaction to the incredible and unprecedented development and surge in population in the 1830–1850 period.

The Westerly End of Roxbury was primarily farms and open, undeveloped land during the first two centuries after Roxbury was settled by the Puritans in 1630, with the early streets Centre, Baker, and Weld. A burial ground was established off Centre Street in 1683 and is still known as the Westerly Burial Ground, where many of the early settlers were buried rather than at the Eliot Burial Ground in the town center. In 1712, partly as a result of the six-mile distance from the town center at Meeting House Hill, the Second Church in Roxbury was established at Peter's Hill, the present area of Walter Street. This simple wood-framed meetinghouse served the religious needs of the residents of the Westerly End throughout the 18th century until 1773, when a new meetinghouse was built at the corner of Centre and Church Streets. By the mid-19th century, this meetinghouse became an important pulpit; it was here that Rev. Theodore Parker preached his fiery and thought-provoking sermons, which attracted many people, including some of the residents of Brook Farm.

An experiment in utopianism, Brook Farm was established in West Roxbury in the 1840s. The transcendental community was established by Rev. George Ripley as a shareholders corporation where people of all walks of life sought to commune with nature. Brook Farm Institute of Agriculture and Education became renowned locally and afar as the place where Nathaniel Hawthorne, Margaret Fuller, and others sought refuge from a changing world. Although the experiment in West Roxbury was short (1841–1847), Brook Farm is still remembered as an important and dynamic aspect of 19th-century thought and action.

In 1848, the West Roxbury Branch of the Boston and Providence Railroad (which had opened in 1834) was laid through the town, with depots eventually being opened at Central (Bellevue) Station, Highland, West Roxbury, and Spring Street. These depots provided convenient transportation and allowed the middle class to move out of the inner city and into the suburbs, where they could commute to Boston for business and pleasure. This resulted in the building boom of the 1850–1865 period. In 1856, horse-drawn streetcars began to service West Roxbury, connecting the Dudley Street area of Roxbury to the town of West Roxbury.

The agitation of the Honorable Arthur W. Austin, a Boston attorney and resident, in the 1840s, for the western area of Roxbury to be incorporated as an independent town was largely a reaction to the increased industrialization of Roxbury. The voters cast their ballots, and by a majority, the town of West Roxbury came into existence on May 24, 1851. The new town met alternately at Taft's Tavern in the South Street Crossing (later Roslindale) and the village hall on Thomas Street (in Jamaica Plain) until a town hall was built in 1868 at the junction of Centre and South Streets "for the greatest convenience of the greatest number" of residents of West Roxbury.

The once open lands in West Roxbury became more valuable after the town was officially incorporated in 1851, and both independent developers and companies, such as the West Roxbury Land Company, developed large tracts of land for new streets and house lots. In the 1880–1895 period, the greatest amount of development in the new neighborhood of the city (West Roxbury was annexed to the city of Boston on January 5, 1874) took place, with the construction of large Queen Anne, Shingle, and Colonial Revival houses on the former farms and estates for the emerging middle class.

Eventually, the West Roxbury Branch and the horse-drawn streetcars became augmented by electric streetcars. After 1909, electric streetcars connected to the Forest Hills Station on the Boston Elevated Railway, which had been extended west from the Dudley Street Station, thereby allowing an even greater segment of the city's population to look at West Roxbury as a possible residence. In the period between 1900 and World War II, West Roxbury saw tremendous residential growth, especially with the creation of the Veterans of Foreign Wars Parkway and the development of the West Roxbury Parkway. Lot sales and house building continued unabated in this period. By the 1920s, multiple-family dwellings were introduced to areas such as Washington Street and Spring Street, thereby diversifying the socioeconomic character of West Roxbury. Some families who moved to West Roxbury from the inner city perceived it as going to the other side of the world because it was so rural in comparison.

Today, West Roxbury—which traces its modern development to 1851, when it became an independent town—is a sought-after neighborhood with well-kept streets lined with a variety of architectural styles that appeal to its diverse residents. In fact, one resident said that those living in West Roxbury "all seemed to be working for the good of the community." That effort is obvious today. In fact, it is "a mature community, which has grown from country district to small town, to suburb, to urban neighborhood."

ACKNOWLEDGMENTS

I would like to thank the following, who assisted, either directly or indirectly, in the writing of this book: Lorna Bognanno; Kathleen Kelly Broomer; Janice Chadbourne, Boston Public Library, Fine Arts Department; Dexter; Edward Gordon; Rev. Michael Parise; Fran Perkins; Anthony and Mary Mitchell Sammarco; the West Roxbury Historical Society; the West Roxbury Branch, Boston Public Library; William Varrell; Jennifer Villeneuve, our editor; and Robert J. Murphy, president of the West Roxbury Historical Society, and board members Christopher Kenneally, Judith A. Helper, Marilyn Oberle, William F. Hennesey, Katherine Ryan, Paul R. Campbell, Jeanne Clancy, and Neil Savage.

This view looks up Corey Street (named for Dea. Ebenezer Corey) from Centre Street in 1885. The rural aspect of West Roxbury, seen here with a dirt street, stone walls, and large amounts of open, undeveloped land, was never more evident. The Whittemore House can be seen on the left and the C.L. Morse House on the right, partially hidden by trees. Today, the First Parish Church, Unitarian, is on the left and Fleet Bank on the right.

Chapter 1
EARLY WEST ROXBURY

The old Richards Tavern was built on Centre Street opposite Mount Vernon Street *c.* 1675 by innkeeper Nathaniel Richards. In front of the old inn in this 1880 photograph are members of the Madden family, who had purchased the property in 1866. Today, the West Roxbury post office is on the site (dispensing a different kind of hospitality), as well as Boston Upholstery and Design.

The old Whiting Tavern was built on Centre Street between Temple and Elgin Streets in 1760 by Ebenezer Whiting. A large square inn with a hip roof, the Whiting Tavern was on the road leading from Boston to Providence and was a popular stopping place for travelers. The inn was demolished in 1892, and the site is now occupied by Dr. Michael J. Lowney's medical office and RE/MAX.

The William Draper House was built *c.* 1720 at 1721 Centre Street on a ledge between what is now Manthorne Road and the West Roxbury Parkway. Captain Draper served in the American Revolution, commanding the 2nd Company of Minutemen at Lexington, but was killed in the Battle of Ticonderoga. Today, a one-story commercial block occupies the site of the house, which was demolished in 1922.

The Judson Chapin House was located at 2003 Centre Street adjacent to the Westerly Burial Ground and near Chapin Avenue. The photograph below captures the picturesque quality of the area *c.* 1874, when West Roxbury was annexed to the city of Boston. A long low stone wall and a fanciful picket fence separate the property from Centre Street, and a massive elm tree shades the five-bay Colonial house. The house was later owned by Frank Hewins but is today the site of Walgreens, with a large parking lot surrounding the store.

The Dr. Abijah Draper House was at 1898 Centre Street at the corner of Park Street and was an elegant five-bay center-entrance Federal house. With the encroachment of commercial development, the house was demolished in 1905. Draper was said to be a "sympathetic friend in sickness and a true friend in need" and was a second-generation doctor in town. Today, Shoes and More and the Irish Cottage stores are on the site.

The Benjamin Guild House was at 2047 Centre Street between Elgin and La Grange Streets and was an interesting house with a center entrance flanked by paired windows on either side, but only three windows were above the entrance. Today, the site is occupied by a modern one-story office block.

In this view looking up Centre Street from Corey Street in 1880, Dr. Abijah Draper's house can be seen on the left at the corner of Centre and Park Streets. The rural aspects of Centre Street in the late 19th century was accented by stone walls, picket fences, and large trees that gracefully shaded the street. Today, Centre Street is a busy thoroughfare with shops on both sides of the street.

The junction of Beech Street, in the foreground, and Anawan Avenue seems like a country crossroads in the 1880s. The area was laid out after the Civil War by the Anawan Land Company and was rapidly built up. Today, the center of the intersection is bisected by the West Roxbury Parkway, a busy four-lane highway that cuts a wide swath through Roslindale and West Roxbury.

The Theodore Parker House, built in 1800 by John Whiting, was at the corner of Centre Street and Cottage Avenue. Here the famous Unitarian minister of the Second Church in Roxbury lived with his wife and his wife's aunt, a Mrs. Cabot. Today, the monumental Maginnis and Walsh–designed St. Theresa of Avila Church is on the site of the old parsonage.

Dr. Abijah Draper's house was at 1898 Centre Street at the corner of Park Street. In the 1880 photograph, the house looks as if it were in the middle of the countryside, with large trees, a barn, carriage house, and wooden fences. Today, the corner features a Family Dollar in a one-story commercial building.

In this view looking west from the corner of Centre and La Grange Streets in 1880, the Benjamin Billings House can be seen on the left. Centre Street, known as the county highway leading to Dedham and thence to Providence, Rhode Island, was a bucolic and tree-lined street in the 19th century. On the right can be seen the Westerly Burial Ground, which was laid out in 1683 in the Westerly End of Roxbury.

In this 1875 view looking west on Centre Street from the corner of La Grange Street, the graceful curve of the street is enhanced by stately trees. On the left is the Benjamin Billings (later Samuel Dana) House, and on the right is the fence in front of the Abner Guild House. Today, a one-story commercial block follows that graceful curve on the left.

The Morse House was at 15 Spring Street, near the corner of Temple Street, and was typical of the early-19th-century houses in this section of West Roxbury. Standing in front of the stone wall is James Morse (1815–1897), a son of the man who built the house c. 1810. Today, Valvoline has a service garage on the site.

The Walker House, located at the corner of Centre and Mount Vernon Streets, was built by John and Lydia Walker *c.* 1860. Seen below *c.* 1891, Lydia Walker stands at the end of the carriage drive with Edward Jordan, her grandson. Today, City Lock is on the corner lot.

The house on the right was at the corner of Centre and Park Streets and was an interesting early-19th-century house with two-story porches and an overhanging roof, giving it the characteristic of a plantation house from the Caribbean. On the left is the Keith-Welsh House (at 1911 Centre Street), a Greek Revival house built *c*. 1840 and now Gilmore Realty. The corner now has the Peoples Federal Savings Bank.

The Second Church in Roxbury was established in 1712, and the meetinghouse was located on Peter's Hill in the Westerly section of Roxbury. This meetinghouse, with its prominent spire that can be seen from South and Centre Streets, was built in 1773 and was the pulpit of the fiery orator Theodore Parker, who preached here in the mid-19th century. Used until 1890, it is today the site of the Church of the Holy Name.

Chapter 2

PLACES OF WORSHIP

The First Parish Church, Unitarian, in West Roxbury was built in 1890 and is the successor to the old Second Church in Roxbury. Designed by noted architect Alexander Wadsworth Longfellow of Longfellow, Alden & Harlow and enlarged by Henry Seaver, the stone church, with its prominent crenelated corner tower, is at the corner of Centre and Corey Streets and has a bronze statue of Rev. Theodore Parker, former pastor of the church, gracing the front lawn.

The First Parish Church in West Roxbury built the present place of worship in 1890 at the corner of Centre and Corey Streets. The church has seven windows designed by Louis Comfort Tiffany and the Tiffany Studios that were installed as memorial windows between 1894 and 1927. Seen here in 1905, the stone church has a prominent corner site. Today, it is in the midst of a busy commercial streetscape. The once open corner in the foreground is now Fleet Bank.

First Parish Unitarian Church, West Roxbury, Mass.

A bronze statue of Rev. Theodore Parker was sculpted by Robert Kraus and placed in 1902 on a granite plinth in front of the First Parish Church on Centre Street. Although he preached in the old meetinghouse on Peter's Hill, at the corner of Centre and Church Streets, he is fondly remembered by the congregation, and the church is often referred to as "the Parker Church." On the left can be seen a corner of the Shaw School on Hastings Street.

The Emmanuel Episcopal Church was designed by Rev. Herman Gaylord Wood and built in 1893 at the corner of Stratford Street and Clement Avenue. The land had been donated to the parish by William Blakemore, a real estate developer, and the stone church was augmented by a parish house, designed by J. Lawrence Berry of Allen & Collens. Reverend Wood designed over 30 Episcopal churches in the United States and was rector of a church in Winthrop.

The West Roxbury Congregational Church was a large Shingle-style church built in 1891 at the corner of Centre and Mount Vernon Streets, on the site of the Old South Evangelical Church. The church had a large bell tower with an interesting roof, along with a four-sided clock that could be seen from all directions. Today, the site of the now demolished church is the new wing of the West Roxbury Branch of the Boston Public Library.

The Daniel Dorchester Memorial (later the Wesley Memorial) Methodist Episcopal Church was designed by Boston architect Oscar A. Thayer and built in 1904 at the corner of Park and March Streets. Using stone, wood shingling, and post–Medieval wattle and daub, it is an interesting late-Victorian design. The church was named for Rev. Daniel Dorchester, who lived at 32 Maxfield Street and preached at United Methodist Church in Roslindale. Today, the St. Matthew's Syrian Orthodox Church worships here.

St. Theresa of Avila Church, seen here in 1895, was originally a wood-framed church built on Spring Street as a mission of St. Mary's Church in Dedham and later Sacred Heart in Roslindale. Eventually, the congregation outgrew this church and a large modern Gothic church, designed by Maginnis and Walsh, was built in 1930 at the corner of Centre Street and St. Theresa Avenue, just a short distance from the original church.

The first schoolhouse in West Roxbury was a small one-room building that was erected in 1767 on land donated by Jeremiah Richards, who gave it "in consideration of my good will and respect, to the proprietors and inhabitants of the westerly end of Roxbury . . . for the use of a school." Built by Nathaniel Whitney, the schoolhouse served generations of local schoolchildren until 1852, after which it was used for sundry purposes, including a two-car garage in the 20th century.

Chapter 3
ASSORTED
SCHOOLS

The old Baker Street School was a one-room wood-framed school built in 1855 at the corner of Baker and Gardner Streets and was typical of the schoolhouses built throughout the area. This schoolhouse had but one teacher, who taught numerous students until it was closed for a larger school. This small schoolhouse was demolished in 1936; the Henry Vane School (on the right) is now used by Catholic Memorial as Donahue Hall.

The old Robert Gould Shaw School was built in 1892 and named for the Civil War hero and colonel of Company 54, the first African American regiment. Born in West Roxbury, Robert Gould Shaw (1837–1863) and 225 of his troops made the supreme sacrifice to the Union when their attack on Fort Wagner in 1863 failed. The school was on Hastings Street between 39 (on the far left) and 15–17 Hastings Street and was later renamed the Olney School. A condominium complex was built on the site in 1988.

The present Robert Gould Shaw School was built at the corner of Mount Vernon Street and Chapin Avenue near the site of the Mount Vernon Street School and was designed by the Boston architectural firm of Blackall, Clapp & Whittemore. The school has seen extensive remodeling over the last few decades, including new windows cut through the brick facades, but the same iron fence still surrounds the property.

The Henry Vane School was built in 1899 on Baker Street next to the old Baker Street Schoolhouse on a part of the old Gardner Estate. An impressive red-brick building, it had stepped gables in the Dutch style and a large arched entrance. The school was named for Sir Henry Vane (1612–1662), a governor of the Massachusetts Bay Colony. Today, this building is part of Catholic Memorial and is known as Donahue Hall.

The Parental School was established on the former Bolles Estate by the city of Boston for young male juvenile delinquents. It was located on Spring Street between Webster Avenue and the Charles River in West Roxbury. The large red-brick and limestone building was designed by Edmund March Wheelewright, the Boston city architect, and built in 1892. Today, the site of the school is the West Roxbury Division of the Department of Veterans Affairs Medical Center. (Author's collection.)

The approach to the Highland Station of the West Roxbury Branch of the Boston and Providence Railroad is seen in this 1905 postcard with a horse-drawn carriage on the right and a new horseless carriage on the left, showing the changes that revolutionized transportation in the early 20th century.

Chapter 4

TRANSPORTATION

The Highland Station on the West Roxbury Branch of the Boston and Providence Railroad was an interesting stone waiting room and passenger depot. It was located behind Centre Street and is seen here in 1890 from the bridge over the tracks on Park Street. Notice the horse and carriage on the left under the porte-cochere and the interesting stepped gable built of locally quarried stone.

The West Roxbury Station on the West Roxbury Branch of the Boston and Providence Railroad was on La Grange Street at the corner of Jordan (later Dent) Street. As seen in this 1895 view looking toward Centre Street, the railroad tracks were at grade, which always caused traffic to stop at the railroad crossing as the train approached. On the left is Chapin Avenue, and on the right is Jordan Street.

The West Roxbury Station was rebuilt in 1899, and the railroad tracks were raised to pass over the street to avoid the increased street traffic of that period. The ticket office and waiting room are on the left, and a covered waiting area is on the right. Today, this is the West Roxbury commuter rail station.

An open electric streetcar passes the corner of Centre and Corey Streets *c.* 1905. The new Highland Club of West Roxbury is in the distance. The streetcar, now replaced by a modern MBTA bus, provided transportation along Centre and Spring Streets and connected West Roxbury to Forest Hills Station. A modern two-story professional building now occupies the site of the Highland Club.

A streetcar bound for the Forest Hills Station on the Boston Elevated Railway turns onto Centre Street from Spring Street in 1947. Between 1880 and 1920, the streetcars, with their nickel fare and ease of transportation, were one of the major reasons new residents moved to West Roxbury. In the distance can be seen a one-story commercial block, 2093–2105 Centre Street, at the corner of Temple Street.

In this view looking toward Corey Street on Centre Street in 1972, the crenelated spire of the First Parish Church dominates the curve of the street as traffic passes in both directions. By this time, Centre Street had become the main shopping area for West Roxbury, just before suburban malls began to draw customers away from the shopping districts of the neighborhoods.

In a view looking west on Centre Street in 1914, the West Roxbury firehouse can be seen on the left at Bellevue Street, with a horse-drawn wagon passing in front of the doors. A wagon on the right pauses in front of the West Roxbury Branch of the Boston Public Library and the West Roxbury Congregational Church at the corner of Centre and Mount Vernon Streets. Today, the firehouse is opposite Osco Drug.

This 1914 view, looking west on Centre Street at Corey Street, shows the First Parish Church on the right, with the roof and chimneys of the Highland Club on the left. In the center is the old Highland Club at the corner of Centre and Hastings Streets. After a new clubhouse was built across the street, the building became the police station. The horse-drawn delivery wagon on the right is from Ware's Milk Company.

Chapter 5

A STREETSCAPE EVOLVES

In this century-old view of the junction of Centre and La Grange Streets, horse-drawn delivery wagons are parked beside the Frost Brothers store. In the center is the Abner Guild House. Today, this section of Centre Street has one-story commercial blocks and is dominated by the crenelated spire of St. Theresa of Avila Church, seen in the distance.

The junction of Spring and Centre Streets, seen here in 1914, was open, with houses on Temple Street on the left. On the right is the wooden fence of the Richard Codman Estate, which was later purchased for the campus of the Roxbury Latin School, the oldest preparatory school in the country. Today, a one-story commercial block is at Centre and Temple Streets, and the school grounds are banked with tall conifers.

The junction of Spring and Centre Streets was directly opposite the Richard Codman Estate, which was at the corner of Cottage Avenue, now St. Theresa Avenue. The bucolic estate was later purchased by the trustees of the Roxbury Latin School, and the school moved here in the 1920s, after their property in Roxbury was sold. The campus was designed by the noted architectural firm of Perry, Shaw and Hepburn.

In this view looking west on Centre Street toward Spring Street, which curves at the right, the fence on the left is that of the old Theodore Parker House at Cottage Avenue, now known as St. Theresa Avenue. The Richard Codman Estate, which later became the campus of the Roxbury Latin School, is seen just beyond.

Centre Street, seen from Cottage Avenue to La Grange Street in 1914, was heavily rutted with streetcar tracks in the center. Seen are the houses of Abner Guild (on the right) and Joseph Billings (on the left). On the far right is a corner of the fence to the estate of Atherton Tilden.

In this 1914 view looking toward Boston is Centre Street. The Westerly Burial Ground is on the left just past the house. A streetcar heads west on Centre Street on its way to Spring Street. Today, Centre Street is lined with one-story commercial blocks.

Looking downhill on Centre Street, at the corner of Mount Vernon Street on the right, this 1914 view shows the old Richards Tavern on the left, just beyond the fence at the railroad tracks. The view today is dominated by the crenelated spire of St. Theresa of Avila Church.

S een here is Centre Street, with Maple Street on the right. One hundred years ago, Centre Street was charming, with 19th-century houses interspersed with early-20th-century houses. Today, this area of Centre Street is almost entirely commercial blocks.

As seen in this 1914 view looking toward Maple Street, Centre Street at Willow Street had a large amount of undeveloped land. On the right is a small one-room waiting station for the streetcar headed toward Forest Hills Station on the elevated railway.

The stone wall in front of the Westerly Burying Ground (on the far left) ran along Centre Street. In this view looking north toward Mount Vernon Street (on the left), the Chapin House and the Cowin House can be seen just beyond the burial ground. Today, the parking lot of Walgreens occupies the area on the left.

In this view looking toward Mount Vernon Street, Centre Street passes over the railroad tracks of the West Roxbury Branch of the Boston and Providence Railroad. Seen in 1914, streetcar tracks run along Centre Street, which has a slight decline as it approaches La Grange Street. On the right is the Mary Draper Memorial of the Daughters of the American Revolution, which was a granite horse trough for passing horses to refresh themselves. Today, the West Roxbury post office is on the left, and the library on the right.

embers of the Hoyt family, along
with their faithful dog, pose in
front of their home at the corner of
Ivory and Temple Streets in the early
20th century. A large Shingle-style
house, the Hoyt home has a gambrel-
gabled facade and Palladian window,
with an impressive shingled archway
spanning the entrance to the piazza,
which is echoed by smaller arches on
the side porch.

Chapter 6

RESIDENTIAL
ARCHITECTURE

Spring Street, at the junction of Aleric Street, was undergoing street excavations in 1898, as the grade was being changed for the bridge at the Spring Street Station. On the left is the Whalen House, and on the far right is the train that serviced the West Roxbury Branch of the Boston and Providence Railroad.

Seen in 1950, the building at 1905–1907 Centre Street was at the corner of Park Street. Built in the early 19th century, it was a duplex house that had a two-story porch and an overhanging roof that echoed architecture from the Caribbean islands or the American South rather than New England. Today, the Peoples Federal Savings Bank is on the site.

In this *c.* 1953 view looking toward Park Street, Centre Street has a Mobil gas station on the left. On the right is Osborne Welsh's house (at 1911 Centre Street) and 1905–1907 Centre Street, which was occupied by the Wildes and Smith families. The building at 1911 Centre Street had been constructed *c.* 1850 by William Keith, a grocer, and was moved back in 1919 for the widening of Centre Street.

The Warren Stokes House was located at 1850 Centre Street, near Corey Lane and adjacent to the Highland Railroad Station. The house was originally owned by Ada T. Hayden but was sold by the Stokes family, and by the 1920s, the land had been developed for commercial use. Today, the Sovereign Bank is on the site.

Temple Street, seen here in 1891, was laid out between Centre Street and Baker Street. On the left is 115 Temple Street, the Spear House, and on the right is 99 Temple Street, the Sumner Osgood House. The vacant lot was purchased by Henry Everett in 1891, and he built his home, now 107 Temple Street, in 1891–1892.

The William S. Mitchell House was at 33 Farrington Avenue, at Anawan Avenue. Mitchell was a successful lumber merchant, building supplier, and hardware dealer who built this Stick-style house *c.* 1880. Today, the former house has been remodeled for commercial purposes, with a large addition on the former facade of the house.

Jason Bailey had an estate on Corey Street that extended back to Mount Vernon Street along Garfield Avenue. The estate was extensive, and the house, a large Shingle-style, stone–and–wood house with a massive rounded bay and a conical roof, was at 200 Centre Street. In the mid-20th century, the estate was subdivided, and Frencroft, Rustlewood, and Grayfield Roads were laid out. Small one-family houses were built on the developed land.

The Everett House was a wood-framed Italianate house built by the Everett family in the 1870s at 246 Park Street. In the 1890 photograph, Henry Everett poses in front of his house before moving to a new house he had built at 107 Temple Street, after Morse's Field had been subdivided for house lots.

Charles M. Seaver built this large Shingle-style house in 1881 at 156 Bellevue Street, originally known as Lyon Street. A large house with an asymmetrical entrance porch, octagonal bay, and interesting windows, it had the necessary carriage house, seen on the right, for the family horse and carriage.

Park Street, as seen in this view looking from Centre Street, had large one- and two-family houses that were built at the turn of the century, set back from the sidewalk and evenly spaced. On the left, a mother and her daughter pass the Moulton House, at 75 Park Street. On the right is 78 Park Street. Notice that the wooden fence has been replaced by a stone wall.

Park Street, West of Centre Street, West Roxbury, Mass.

Maple Street, originally known as Fruit Street, is seen from Centre Street. Large houses were built on Maple Street at the turn of the century. On the left is 16 Maple Street, and on the right are 5 and 15 Maple Street. Today, Espresso Pizza occupies the corner, and large shade trees mask the residential architecture.

Maxfield Street was laid out in 1891 and connects La Grange and Bellevue Streets. Laid through the former estate of Joseph H. Billings, Maxfield Street had large Victorian houses built at the turn of the century, with smaller infill houses during the mid-20th century. Billings Field was once part of the estate and remains open as a park today.

xfield St. West Roxbury, Mass.   643

The house at 43 Stratford Street was built by the Pierce family, who also built the Pierce Block at 1870–1876 Centre Street. A large center-entrance Colonial Revival house with matching swell-bay facades, the house had an overhanging dormered hip roof, bracketed cornice, and front piazza. In 1912, the house was purchased by the J.S.D. Everett family, who had lived on Vermont Street.

The Whittemore House was built by Harry L. Whittemore at 1977 Centre Street, near the intersection with Mount Vernon Street. A large Colonial Revival house with a center-entrance porch, paired Doric columns, a rounded bay, and a dormered hip roof and balustrades, it attested to his success as a milk trader in West Roxbury, Roslindale, and Jamaica Plain at the turn of the century. Today, the site is the parking lot of Friendly's.

Gray photo

Hastings Street, West Roxbury, Mass.

In this view looking up Hastings Street from Centre Street, on the left is a corner of 44–46 Hastings Street and 48–50 Hastings Street next door. Hastings Street was laid out in 1892 and developed with one- and two-family houses at the turn of the century. The houses were all within walking distance of the train at the Highland Station.

Sears Gallagher built his house at 307 La Grange Street. A noted etcher and watercolor artist and member of the Boston school, Gallagher (1896–1955) commissioned Boston architect George E. Barton in 1897 to design his house, which was a large Shingle- and Tudor-style house at the corner of La Grange and Fernwood Road.

MASS
HOME OF THE
BEAN AND THE COD

BOSTON
TRAILER PARK
INC.
ROUTE I, BOSTON
West Roxbury District

TRAILER SALES

U. S. HIGHWAY I
On The Scenic Charles River
8 Miles South of Boston, Massachusetts

OFFICE

The Boston Trailer Park is at 1515 Veterans of Foreign Wars Parkway (Route 1), on the former site of Caledonian Grove, a recreation area at the turn of the century. Opened by the Aders after World War II, the trailer park offered such amenities as sewer connections, tiled showers, and an automatic laundry. Today, adjacent to Clair Buick, the Boston Trailer Park is still the only one of its kind in the city.

In this early-20th-century view, Charles Kelley poses for a photograph at the corner of Temple and Ivory Streets in his horse-drawn delivery wagon of the West Roxbury Ice Company. Ice was harvested at Cow Island Pond on the Charles River and stored in icehouses that stood on the present site of the Metropolitan District Commission skating rink. Prior to electric refrigeration, ice was delivered to local homes and placed in iceboxes to keep food cool.

Chapter 7
A NEIGHBORHOOD CALLED WEST ROXBURY

In 1875, William S. Mitchell established a lumber and building supply yard on Beech Street near Anawan Avenue at the West Roxbury Parkway. Seen in 1890, employees of the lumber and hardware concern pose for a photograph in front of the store's office. Mitchell lived at 33 Farrington Avenue and was a major supplier of lumber used in the building boom in West Roxbury between 1875 and 1910. Today, the former site of the lumber and supply yard is private property.

The corner of Centre and La Grange Streets had the G.A. Newhall store (on the left) and the Billings sheepskin factory (on the right). Today, Blanchard's (a liquor store) and remnants of the old Billings factory occupy the corners.

Anawan Hall was on Anawan Avenue at the head of Belgrade Avenue and was a large Victorian commercial building built *c.* 1875, with stores on the first floor and a large hall on the second floor. The area was laid out in the 1870s by the Anawan Land Company, and Anawan Hall was located near Central Station (later Bellevue Station) on the West Roxbury Branch of the Boston and Providence Railroad. The house on the left is on Anawan Street near the West Roxbury Parkway. Howard Chevrolet occupies the site today.

The Pierce Block was built by Dr. Frank D. Pierce at 1872 Centre Street and was a two-story commercial building with shops on the first floor and professional offices above, accessible via the center entrance and a staircase. On the far left is a corner of the Highland Club, which was on the corner of Corey Street.

Gordon Hall was built by John Gordon in 1898 at the corner of Spring and Summer Streets. An interesting Colonial Revival building, it had stores on the first floor with a large hall on the second floor. Notice the exaggerated Colonial Revival details, such as the broken arch finials, swagged lintels, and arched windows. Today, two large three-deckers occupy the site.

In this 1910 view looking toward Richwood Street, Centre Street has a gentle curve. A streetcar heads west and passes the Highland Club (later the police station) as it heads toward Spring Street at the Charles River from the Dudley Street terminal.

The West Roxbury firehouse for Engine 30 and Ladder 25 was designed by Boston city architect Edmund March Wheelwright and was built at 1940 Centre Street near Bellevue Street. A large red-brick and brownstone Romanesque Revival firehouse, it is distinguished by Diocletian windows and rusticated entry surrounds.

Built as the first home of the popular Highland Club, at the corner of Centre and Hastings Street, this became the police headquarters after the club built a new clubhouse across the street. A large Shingle-style clubhouse, it had a front piazza that wrapped around the front and side and a large flagpole on the corner. Today, the site is used as a parking lot.

The West Roxbury Division, Department of Veterans Affairs Medical Center, seen here in 1952, was built at the corner of American Legion Highway and Spring Street. A large red-brick and cement Colonial Revival building, now known as Building No. 1, it was built on the site of the Parental School for Truants.

The Highland Club built a new Colonial Revival clubhouse at the corner of Centre and Corey Streets and dedicated it in 1902. Its four Ionic columns and elegant architectural details were enjoyed less than six decades, as the clubhouse was demolished in 1965, and a modern two-story office building was built on its site.

The West Roxbury Branch of the Boston Public Library was originally located on the first floor of the former Westerly Hall on Centre Street, adjacent to the West Roxbury Congregational Church. Westerly Hall was later replaced by the Mount Vernon School, which had been on the site of the present Shaw School. Notice the Mary Draper Memorial of the Daughters of the American Revolution in front, which was a granite horse trough. Today, this is the older portion of the library.

The West Roxbury Free Library (successor to the Spring Street Social Library) is seen below in 1878. It was located in Westerly Hall, a two-story wood-framed Italianate building on Centre Street, the present site of the library. Young students pose in rigid formation in front of the building, which also acted as the primary school on the second floor, above the library. In 1922, Westerly Hall was moved across the street and was later demolished.

The West Roxbury Branch of the Boston Public Library was designed by Oscar A. Thayer (1870–1950) and built in 1922 on Centre Street, adjacent to the West Roxbury Congregational Church, seen on the left. An impressive Georgian Revival library, it was the successor to the West Roxbury Free Library, which had been founded in 1863.

The West Roxbury Branch of the Boston Public Library can be seen on the left in 1948. The house on the right was later demolished and is now the site of the CVS drugstore and parking lot.

Seen here in 1952, Centre Street between Park and Bellevue Streets had a number of buildings with stores on the first floor and apartments above. To the center left is a First National supermarket.

In this view looking toward Hastings Street on Centre Street in 1948, the West Roxbury firehouse can be seen on the far right, with the old police station (in the old Highland Club building) on the far left. The wooden buildings had stores on the first floor with apartments above and were later demolished.

The First National Bank of Boston built a new one-story, red-brick branch office in West Roxbury at the corner of Centre and Corey Streets in 1953. Today, Fleet Bank, the successor to the bank, has its modern branch in a remodeled and enlarged building, complete with a parking lot for customers.

Below, Laurence Dolliver poses proudly in front of the Esso gas pumps at the filling station on Spring Street, opposite Summer Street. A Shaw's supermarket is now on the site of the gas station.

Mr. and Mrs. Arthur Hoyt pause for a photograph in their elegant one-horse shay in the early 20th century. The West Roxbury they knew was a rapidly expanding neighborhood with fashionable one-family houses springing up, as if by magic, throughout the area due to the ease of transportation of both streetcars and the West Roxbury Branch of the Boston and Providence Railroad. A century later, their descendants still view West Roxbury as a comfortable, convenient, and accessible neighborhood of the city of Boston.